Animals

Eagles

by Nick Rebman

FOCUS READERS

FOCUS READERS

www.focusreaders.com

Focus Readers is distributed by North Star Editions:
sales@northstareditions.com | 888-417-0195

Produced for Focus Readers by Red Line Editorial.

Photographs ©: Chris Hill/Shutterstock Images, cover, 1; Carol Gray/Shutterstock Images, 4; critterbiz/Shutterstock Images, 7, 9, 16 (bottom left), 16 (bottom right); Carol Kelpin/Shutterstock Images, 11, 16 (top right); Igor Kovalenko/Shutterstock Images, 13; Teri Virbickis/Shutterstock Images, 15, 16 (top left)

ISBN
978-1-63517-849-4 (hardcover)
978-1-63517-950-7 (paperback)
978-1-64185-153-4 (ebook pdf)
978-1-64185-052-0 (hosted ebook)

Library of Congress Control Number: 2018931097

Printed in the United States of America
Mankato, MN
May, 2018

About the Author

Nick Rebman enjoys reading, drawing, and traveling to places where he doesn't speak the language. He lives in Minnesota.

Table of Contents

Eagles

Eagles have white heads.

Eagles have
brown bodies.

Eagles have yellow legs.

An eagle has **wings**.

An eagle has **claws**.

An eagle has a **beak**.

wing
beak
claw

Behavior

Eagles can fly fast.

Eagles can fly high.

Eagles live in trees.

They make **nests**.

The nests are big.

nest

Food

An eagle flies down to the water.

It grabs a fish.

It eats the fish.

fish

Eagles are large birds.

They can live for 20 years.

Glossary

beak

nests

claws

wings

Index